Be a Champion

Life Changing Ideas to Build Yourself as a Champion

Author: Ghazi Mokammel Hossain

Design: Ghazi Mokammel Hossain

Publications Format: Amazon Kindle E-Book format, Amazon Createspace Paperback format

Edition No: First Edition, (July, 2023)

ISBN: 9798852040169

Publication From: USA (Global Version)

Publisher: GM Publishers, associated with Amazon Kindle Direct Publishing & Createspace

Email address: gmpublishers04@gmail.com

Website: www.gmpublishers.com

https://www.gmpublishers.com/

Table of Contents

1.0 Introduction

Welcome to Be a Champion! This book is for those who aspire to be more, who refuse to settle for mediocrity, and who are willing to step outside their comfort zone to achieve greatness. Whether you're striving for success in your personal or professional life, this book will inspire and guide you on your journey to become a true champion.

A champion is not just someone who wins trophies or earns accolades. Being a champion is a state of mind, a way of life. It's about pushing yourself beyond your perceived limits, overcoming challenges, and consistently striving for excellence. It's about embracing failure as a stepping stone to success and never giving up, even when the odds seem insurmountable.

In these pages, we will explore the mindset, habits, and strategies of champions from various walks of life, including sports, business, arts, and beyond. We will delve into the lessons they've learned, the obstacles they've faced, and the strategies they've employed to achieve their goals. From legendary athletes who have conquered their respective fields to entrepreneurs who have built thriving businesses from scratch, you'll gain insights from their stories and wisdom.

But this book is not just about learning from others. It's about unlocking your own potential and tapping into the champion within you. It's about identifying your strengths, setting ambitious goals, and taking intentional steps to achieve them. It's about developing resilience, discipline, and perseverance to overcome setbacks and keep moving forward.

As you embark on this journey, be prepared to challenge your mindset, confront your fears, and embrace the discomfort of growth. Be ready to push yourself beyond your comfort zone, because that's where real transformation happens. Remember, being a champion is not reserved for a select few; it's a mindset and a way of life that anyone can adopt.

So, are you ready to unleash your potential and strive for greatness? Are you ready to Be a Champion? Let's dive in and start this transformative journey together!

1.1 Prepare Yourself as a Champion

Congratulations on taking the first step towards becoming a champion! In this segment, we will discuss the key guidelines to help you prepare yourself to embrace the champion's mindset and embark on your journey towards greatness. By following these guidelines, you will develop a strong foundation to unleash your potential and achieve your goals.

1. **Set Clear Goals:** Champions know exactly what they want to achieve, and they set clear, measurable, and achievable goals. Take the time to define your short-term and long-term goals, both in your personal and professional life. Write them down and revisit them regularly to stay focused and motivated.

2. **Cultivate a Positive Mindset:** Your mindset plays a crucial role in your success. Champions cultivate a positive and growth-oriented mindset. Believe in yourself, your abilities, and your potential to achieve greatness. Embrace challenges as opportunities for growth, and adopt a "can-do" attitude. Surround yourself with positive influences and eliminate negativity from your life.

3. **Develop Resilience:** Champions face setbacks and obstacles, but they don't give up. They bounce back stronger and learn from failures. Develop resilience by embracing challenges, staying persistent, and maintaining a positive outlook in the face of

adversity. Use failures as learning opportunities and keep moving forward towards your goals.

4. **Cultivate Discipline:** Champions understand the importance of discipline in achieving their goals. Develop discipline by setting routines, managing your time effectively, and staying committed to your goals. Learn to prioritize tasks, avoid distractions, and stay focused on what matters most.

5. **Continuously Learn and Improve:** Champions never stop learning and improving. Seek opportunities for growth and development. Stay curious, be open to feedback, and constantly strive to enhance your skills and knowledge. Embrace a growth mindset and be willing to step out of your comfort zone to learn and improve.

6. **Build a Support System:** Champions don't achieve greatness alone. Surround yourself with a supportive network of mentors, coaches, peers, and friends who will encourage and inspire you. Seek guidance from those who have walked the path before you and learn from their experiences.

7. **Take Care of Your Physical and Mental Well-being:** Your physical and mental health are critical to your success. Champions prioritize self-care by taking care of their physical health through regular exercise, proper nutrition, and adequate rest. They also prioritize their mental health by managing stress, practicing self-compassion, and seeking help when needed.

8. **Embrace Continuous Effort and Perseverance:** Champions understand that success requires continuous effort and perseverance. Be willing to put in the hard work, push through challenges, and

never give up on your dreams. Embrace a "never quit" attitude and stay committed to your goals, even when the going gets tough.

9. **Visualize Success:** Champions use the power of visualization to create a clear mental image of their desired outcome. Visualize yourself achieving your goals, imagine the feeling of success, and use this mental imagery to stay motivated and focused on your journey towards greatness.

10. **Take Action:** Ultimately, becoming a champion requires action. Take consistent and intentional steps towards your goals. Break your goals down into manageable tasks and take action every day, no matter how small. Remember, progress is more important than perfection.

By following these guidelines, you will prepare yourself to embrace the champion's mindset and set yourself up for success. Remember, becoming a champion is a journey, not a destination. Stay committed, stay focused, and never stop believing in yourself. Get ready to unlock your full potential and strive for greatness as you embark on this transformative journey towards becoming a true champion.

1.2 The Lifestyle of a Champion

The lifestyle of a champion goes beyond just achieving success in a particular endeavor; it encompasses a holistic approach to life that is characterized by certain key habits, behaviours, and attitudes. In this segment, we will explore the lifestyle of a champion in depth, providing insights and guidelines for you to adopt and integrate into your own life.

1. **Discipline and Consistency:** Champions understand that success requires discipline and consistency. They develop a routine and stick

to it diligently, even when they don't feel like it. They prioritize their goals, manage their time effectively, and make consistent efforts towards their objectives, day in and day out.

2. **Goal-Oriented Mindset:** Champions are driven by clear goals and a strong sense of purpose. They set specific, measurable, achievable, relevant, and time-bound (SMART) goals, and align their actions with these goals. They stay focused on their objectives, and make decisions and take actions that are in line with their desired outcomes.

3. **Continuous Learning and Growth:** Champions have a thirst for knowledge and constantly seek opportunities for learning and growth. They invest in their personal and professional development by reading, attending workshops, taking courses, and seeking feedback. They embrace a growth mindset, view failures as opportunities for learning, and constantly strive to improve themselves.

4. **Mental Resilience:** Champions develop mental toughness to overcome challenges and setbacks. They cultivate resilience by managing stress, staying positive, and maintaining a strong belief in their abilities. They have the ability to bounce back from failures, adapt to changing circumstances, and persevere in the face of adversity.

5. **Healthy Lifestyle:** Champions understand the importance of physical well-being in their overall success. They prioritize their health by maintaining a balanced diet, staying physically active, and getting enough sleep. They take care of their body as it is the vessel

that carries them towards their goals, and they know that a healthy body contributes to a healthy mind.

6. **Passion and Dedication:** Champions are passionate about their pursuits and dedicated to their craft. They have a burning desire to excel in their chosen field and are willing to put in the hard work and effort required. They are persistent, committed, and willing to make sacrifices to achieve their goals.

7. **Positive Relationships:** Champions recognize the value of positive relationships in their lives. They surround themselves with people who support, motivate, and challenge them to be better. They foster healthy relationships with mentors, peers, and other like-minded individuals who inspire and push them towards greatness.

8. **Focus on Excellence, Not Perfection:** Champions understand that perfection is unattainable, and they focus on excellence instead. They strive to do their best in everything they do, aiming for continuous improvement rather than chasing an unattainable ideal. They embrace a growth mindset, learn from mistakes, and constantly seek ways to enhance their performance.

9. **Time for Rest and Recovery:** Champions understand the importance of rest and recovery in maintaining their peak performance. They prioritize self-care and make time for relaxation, leisure activities, and hobbies. They understand that rest is essential for recharging their physical and mental energy, allowing them to perform at their best in the long run.

10. **Giving Back and Inspiring Others:** Champions understand that their success is not just about themselves; it's about making a

positive impact on others and inspiring them to achieve greatness. They give back to their communities, mentor others, and share their knowledge and experiences to help others along their journey towards success.

Incorporating these habits, behaviors, and attitudes into your lifestyle can help you cultivate the mindset of a champion. It's important to note that the lifestyle of a champion is not always easy, and it requires dedication, perseverance, and continuous effort. However, the rewards are immense, as you unlock your full potential and strive for greatness in all aspects

1.3 True Champions are the Religious Persons

The statement "True Champions are the Religious Persons" can be interpreted in different ways, depending on one's perspective and beliefs. In this segment, we will explore the concept of religiosity and its potential relationship with champion-like qualities.

Religiosity, broadly defined, refers to the level of adherence, commitment, and involvement in religious beliefs, practices, and rituals. It can encompass various aspects, such as organized religion, personal spirituality, and faith-based values. While religiosity is often associated with one's relationship with a higher power or a specific religious tradition, it can also be seen as a way of life that influences one's attitudes, behaviors, and outlook on life.

Here are some key points to consider when discussing the potential connection between religiosity and being a true champion:

1. **Faith and Resilience:** Religion can provide a source of faith and hope, which can be a driving force in times of adversity. Believers often draw strength and resilience from their faith during difficult

situations, allowing them to persevere and overcome challenges with a sense of purpose and conviction.

2. **Moral and Ethical Values:** Religion often promotes a set of moral and ethical values that guide believers in their actions and interactions with others. These values, such as compassion, empathy, forgiveness, and justice, can foster a sense of responsibility towards others and contribute to the development of character traits that are often associated with champion-like qualities.

3. **Sense of Purpose and Meaning:** Religion can provide believers with a sense of purpose and meaning in life. It can offer a framework for understanding the world and one's place in it, and provide a sense of direction and motivation towards meaningful goals. It helps us to understand that we are the creations and slaves of Almighty Allah (God) only. This sense of purpose can fuel one's drive to achieve excellence and make a positive impact on others.

4. **Community and Support:** Religious communities often provide a sense of belonging, support, and camaraderie for their members. These communities can foster a supportive environment that encourages personal growth, accountability, and mutual assistance, which can contribute to the development of champion-like qualities such as teamwork, leadership, and resilience.

5. **Humility and Gratitude:** Many religious traditions emphasize humility, gratitude, and reverence towards a higher power or the divine. These virtues can foster a sense of humility and gratitude towards life's blessings, and a recognition of the interconnectedness

of all things. This can promote a mindset of gratitude, humility, and service towards others, which are qualities often associated with champions.

6. **Self-Reflection and Self-Improvement:** Religious practices often involve self-reflection, introspection, and self-improvement. Through practices such as 5 times prayers, meditation, or self-examination, believers are encouraged to reflect on their thoughts, actions, and attitudes, and strive for self-improvement. This self-reflective mindset can contribute to self-awareness, self-mastery, and continuous self-improvement, which are important qualities for personal growth and excellence.

It's important to note that religiosity is a complex and diverse concept, and not all religious persons may embody the qualities typically associated with champions. Additionally, champion-like qualities can also be found in individuals who may not identify as religious. The relationship between religiosity and being a champion is subjective and can vary depending on personal beliefs, experiences, and cultural contexts.

In conclusion, while religiosity may not be a universal characteristic of true champions, it can provide a framework for individuals to cultivate qualities such as faith, resilience, moral values, sense of purpose, community, humility, and self-improvement. It is up to individuals to interpret and integrate these qualities into their own lives, regardless of their religious beliefs or practices. Ultimately, being a true champion involves embodying a set of positive qualities and behaviours that contribute to personal growth, excellence, and making a positive impact on others.

2.0 Don't Follow the Lifestyle of the Celebrities If You Wanna Become a Champion

The lifestyle of celebrities is often glamorized and portrayed as an ideal to aspire to. However, in reality, emulating the lifestyle of celebrities may not necessarily lead to becoming a true champion. In this segment, we will delve into the reasons why following the lifestyle of celebrities may not be conducive to achieving champion-like qualities and success.

1. **Unrealistic Standards:** Celebrities are often depicted in the media as having perfect lives, with seemingly unlimited wealth, fame, and success. However, it's important to remember that this portrayal is often curated and may not reflect the reality of their lives. Trying to live up to the unrealistic standards set by celebrities can lead to feelings of inadequacy, self-comparison, and an unhealthy pursuit of materialistic gains, which may not align with the values and qualities that define true champions.

2. **Superficial Focus:** The lifestyle of celebrities is often centered around external appearances, material possessions, and social status. This can create a superficial focus on external validation, image, and fame, rather than on inner qualities, personal growth, and meaningful contributions to society. True champions, on the other hand, prioritize inner qualities such as character, integrity, resilience, and purpose-driven actions that go beyond superficial appearances.

3. **Lack of Authenticity:** The celebrity culture often promotes a superficial and manufactured image that may not align with authentic self-expression and individuality. Many celebrities are

under constant scrutiny and pressure to conform to societal expectations, which can result in a loss of personal identity and authenticity. Champions, on the other hand, embrace their unique qualities, stay true to their values, and cultivate authenticity in their thoughts, words, and actions.

4. **Focus on Instant Gratification:** The lifestyle of celebrities often promotes a culture of instant gratification, with emphasis on material wealth, fame, and indulgence in hedonistic pleasures. This can foster a mindset of immediate rewards without putting in the necessary hard work, perseverance, and dedication required for achieving long-term success. In contrast, true champions understand the value of patience, discipline, and delayed gratification in pursuing their goals and overcoming challenges.

5. **Lack of Purpose and Meaning:** The lifestyle of celebrities may not always emphasize a sense of purpose and meaning beyond personal gain. Many celebrities may focus primarily on their own success, without a broader perspective on making a positive impact on society or contributing to a greater cause. In contrast, champions often strive for a sense of purpose and meaning in their actions, driven by a desire to create positive change in the world and make a meaningful difference in the lives of others.

6. **Neglect of Personal Well-being:** The lifestyle of celebrities can often be demanding and stressful, with intense pressure, constant scrutiny, and lack of privacy. This can result in neglect of personal well-being, including physical, mental, and emotional health. True champions recognize the importance of self-care, balance, and well-

being as the foundation for sustainable success and excellence in all areas of life.

In conclusion, while the lifestyle of celebrities may seem appealing on the surface, it may not necessarily align with the qualities and values that define true champions. Emulating the lifestyle of celebrities can lead to unrealistic standards, superficial focus, lack of authenticity, focus on instant gratification, lack of purpose and meaning, and neglect of personal well-being.

True champions, on the other hand, prioritize inner qualities, authenticity, purpose-driven actions, delayed gratification, and personal well-being in their pursuit of success and making a positive impact on others and the world around them. It's important to focus on cultivating champion-like qualities that are aligned with our values, personal growth, and positive contributions to society, rather than blindly following the lifestyle of celebrities.

3.0 Follow the Paths of Prophets in Islam if You Wanna Become a True Champion

In Islam, the Prophets (peace be upon them) hold a special status as exemplary role models for Muslims. They are revered for their righteousness, wisdom, leadership, and unwavering faith in Almighty Allah (God). Following the paths of the Prophets can serve as a guide for Muslims who aspire to become true champions in various aspects of their lives. In this segment, we will delve into the reasons why emulating the Prophets in Islam can be a source of inspiration and guidance for becoming a true champion.

1. **Divine Guidance:** The Prophets in Islam were chosen by Allah as messengers to convey His guidance to humanity. They received

divine revelations and followed the commandments of Allah in their lives. Emulating the Prophets means following the divine guidance they received and applying it in our own lives. This includes following the teachings of the Quran, the holy book of Islam, and the Hadith, the sayings and actions of the Prophet Muhammad (peace be upon him). By following the paths of the Prophets, Muslims can align their actions and beliefs with the guidance of Allah, which can lead to a righteous and purpose-driven life.

2. **Moral and Ethical Excellence:** The Prophets in Islam exemplified high moral and ethical standards in their actions and interactions with others. They displayed traits such as honesty, kindness, patience, humility, forgiveness, and generosity. Emulating these qualities can help Muslims develop strong character, integrity, and ethical values, which are crucial for becoming true champions in all aspects of life, including personal, family, social, and professional spheres. Following the paths of the Prophets can inspire Muslims to strive for moral and ethical excellence in their thoughts, words, and deeds.

3. **Resilience and Perseverance:** The Prophets in Islam faced numerous challenges, trials, and tribulations in their lives, but they displayed unwavering resilience and perseverance in their faith and mission. They remained steadfast in their commitment to Allah and continued to strive for righteousness despite facing adversity. Emulating their resilience and perseverance can inspire Muslims to face challenges with patience, determination, and trust in Allah's wisdom and guidance. This can foster a resilient mindset, enabling

them to overcome obstacles and achieve their goals, which is a crucial quality for becoming a true champion.

4. **Leadership and Advocacy:** The Prophets in Islam were not only spiritual leaders, but also leaders in their communities, advocating for justice, equality, and social welfare. They stood up against injustice, oppression, and ignorance, and worked towards the betterment of society. Emulating their leadership and advocacy can inspire Muslims to become proactive agents of positive change in their communities and beyond. It can instill a sense of responsibility towards promoting social justice, uplifting the marginalized, and advocating for noble causes, which are essential qualities of a true champion.

5. **Empathy and Compassion:** The Prophets in Islam displayed empathy and compassion towards others, including the poor, the needy, the oppressed, and the vulnerable. They showed kindness, mercy, and understanding towards all of Allah's creation. Emulating their empathy and compassion can inspire Muslims to develop a caring and compassionate attitude towards others, to show kindness, and to lend a helping hand to those in need. Such qualities foster harmonious relationships, build social cohesion, and contribute to the well-being of society, which are important aspects of being a true champion.

6. **Continuous Self-Improvement:** The Prophets in Islam were always striving for self-improvement and self-purification. They sought Allah's forgiveness, reflected on their actions, and continuously worked towards self-improvement. Emulating their humility and self-reflection can encourage Muslims to engage in

continuous   self-improvement,   introspection,   and   self-
accountability.

4.0 Don't Be Disappointed to Lose Any Opportunities in Your Life

Losing opportunities in life can be disappointing and disheartening. It can make us feel like we have failed or missed out on something important. However, in this segment, we will explore why it is essential not to be overly disappointed when we lose opportunities, but instead, view them as valuable learning experiences that can contribute to our growth and eventual success.

1. **Opportunity for Learning:** Losing opportunities can be valuable learning experiences. It provides us with an opportunity to reflect on our actions, decisions, and strategies. We can analyze what went wrong, identify areas for improvement, and learn from our mistakes. This self-reflection and introspection can help us develop self-awareness, critical thinking, and problem-solving skills. It allows us to learn from our failures and make better-informed choices in the future, ultimately contributing to our personal and professional growth.

2. **Resilience and Character Building:** Facing disappointment and setbacks can build resilience and character. It tests our perseverance, determination, and mental toughness. It challenges us to bounce back from failure, dust ourselves off, and keep moving forward. Overcoming disappointments can foster a resilient mindset, where we learn to handle setbacks with grace and resilience. It can also help develop qualities such as patience, perseverance, and

determination, which are essential for navigating the ups and downs of life and ultimately becoming a stronger, more resilient individual.

3. **New Opportunities May Arise:** Losing one opportunity does not mean the end of the road. Often, when one door closes, another one opens. Losing out on one opportunity may lead to the discovery of new opportunities that we may not have otherwise considered. It may force us to explore different paths, think creatively, and take risks. Being open to new possibilities and not getting overly disappointed by losing an opportunity can open doors to new and unexpected opportunities that may even surpass our initial expectations.

4. **Redefining Success:** Losing opportunities can provide us with an opportunity to redefine our understanding of success. It can challenge us to question our preconceived notions of success and what truly matters in life. It can help us reassess our values, priorities, and goals. Losing out on one opportunity may lead us to realize that there are other aspects of our lives that are equally or even more important, such as our health, relationships, or personal well-being. It can help us shift our focus from external validation to inner fulfilment and contentment, which can lead to a more holistic and fulfilling sense of success.

5. **Motivation to Improve:** Losing opportunities can also serve as a motivation to improve ourselves and strive for better. It can ignite a fire within us to work harder, be more prepared, and seize future opportunities with renewed vigor. It can help us set higher standards for ourselves, push our boundaries, and continuously strive for excellence. Losing out on an opportunity can be a catalyst for self-

improvement and self-motivation, propelling us towards our goals with increased determination and commitment.

6. **Building Resilient Mindset:** Losing opportunities can be seen as a part of the journey towards success rather than a roadblock. It can teach us to embrace failure as a natural part of life and develop a resilient mindset. Instead of getting overly disappointed and discouraged, we can learn to see failures as stepping stones towards success. We can learn to bounce back from setbacks, adapt to challenges, and keep moving forward with unwavering determination and optimism.

In conclusion, losing opportunities in life can be disappointing, but it is important to view them as valuable learning experiences that contribute to our personal and professional growth. It can build resilience, character, and self-improvement, and open doors to new opportunities. By maintaining a positive mindset, embracing failures as part of the journey, and learning from our mistakes, we can turn disappointments into opportunities for growth

5.0 True Champions Adopt the Normal Lifestyle Over the Luxurious Lifestyle

Living a normal lifestyle, rather than a luxurious one, can be a defining characteristic of true champions. In today's society, there is often a glorification of wealth, luxury, and material possessions. However, in this segment, we will explore why adopting a normal lifestyle, focused on simplicity, humility, and meaningful values, can lead to greater fulfillment and success in the long run.

1. **Focus on Substance Over Appearances:** True champions understand that a meaningful life is not solely about material wealth or extravagant luxuries. They recognize that real fulfillment comes from within and is not solely reliant on external possessions or status symbols. Instead of chasing superficial pleasures, they prioritize substance over appearances. They invest their time, energy, and resources in cultivating meaningful relationships, personal growth, and contributing to their communities. By focusing on what truly matters, they are able to build a more fulfilling and purpose-driven life.

2. **Humility and Gratitude:** Champions who adopt a normal lifestyle often possess humility and gratitude. They do not get caught up in the pursuit of extravagant possessions or showing off their wealth. They are grateful for the simple pleasures in life and do not take things for granted. They recognize that material possessions are temporary and do not define their worth or success. Instead, they appreciate the little joys, such as spending time with loved ones, pursuing their passions, and making a positive impact on others. Humility and gratitude keep them grounded, humble, and appreciative of life's blessings.

3. **Focus on Personal Development:** Champions who embrace a normal lifestyle prioritize personal development over materialistic pursuits. They invest in self-improvement, continuous learning, and skill development. They recognize that true success comes from within and that they are their most valuable asset. Rather than relying solely on external factors, they work on honing their skills, expanding their knowledge, and developing their character. They

are constantly striving to be the best version of themselves and grow in all aspects of their lives.

4. **Financial Responsibility and Freedom:** Living a normal lifestyle also involves being financially responsible and having the freedom to make choices based on values rather than material desires. Champions who adopt a normal lifestyle understand the importance of financial literacy, budgeting, and wise financial management. They do not succumb to the temptations of excessive spending or living beyond their means. Instead, they prioritize financial stability, savings, and investments that align with their long-term goals. By being financially responsible, they gain the freedom to make choices based on their values and priorities, rather than being driven solely by materialistic desires.

5. **Authenticity and Integrity:** True champions who embrace a normal lifestyle prioritize authenticity and integrity in their actions and decisions. They do not feel the need to put on a façade or impress others with material possessions. They are true to themselves and live in alignment with their values and beliefs. They do not compromise their integrity or values for the sake of fleeting luxuries. They understand that true success is built on a foundation of authenticity, integrity, and genuine connections with others.

6. **Focus on Meaningful Impact:** Champions who embrace a normal lifestyle often have a greater focus on making a meaningful impact on the world around them. They recognize that life is not just about personal gains, but also about contributing positively to society. They engage in acts of kindness, give back to their communities, and work towards making a positive difference in the lives of others.

They find fulfillment in making a meaningful impact rather than solely pursuing materialistic pleasures.

In conclusion, adopting a normal lifestyle, focused on simplicity, humility, and meaningful values. This can be a defining characteristic of true champions. It allows them to prioritize substance over appearances, cultivate humility and gratitude, focus on personal development, be financially responsible, prioritize authenticity and integrity, and make a meaningful impact on the world around them.

5.1 True Champions are the Selfless Persons

Selflessness is a key characteristic of true champions. While the world often celebrates individual success and personal achievements, true champions understand that selflessness and altruism are essential qualities that lead to greater fulfillment and success in the long run. In this segment, we will delve into why selflessness is a vital attribute of true champions and how it contributes to their overall success and impact.

1. **Service to Others:** True champions prioritize serving others above their own interests. They are willing to lend a helping hand, extend kindness, and make sacrifices to assist those in need. They understand that true success is not just about personal achievements, but also about making a positive impact on the lives of others. By selflessly serving others, they build meaningful relationships, foster a sense of community, and create a positive ripple effect that can inspire and motivate others to do the same.

2. **Empathy and Compassion:** Champions who are selfless possess a deep sense of empathy and compassion towards others. They are able to understand and connect with the emotions, struggles, and

needs of those around them. They listen with an open heart, show understanding, and offer support without any expectation of personal gain. Their compassion and empathy enable them to be a source of comfort, encouragement, and inspiration to those who may be going through challenges.

3. **Collaborative Spirit:** True champions understand the power of collaboration and teamwork. They are willing to collaborate with others, share credit, and work towards a common goal without seeking personal glory. They believe in the strength of collective efforts and recognize that true success often requires the contributions of many. They are willing to share their knowledge, skills, and resources with others, and celebrate the success of the team as a whole rather than just their individual achievements.

4. **Humility and Gratitude:** Selfless champions possess humility and gratitude. They do not boast about their achievements or seek constant recognition. They don't assist others for the initial recognition and personal gain.

   They are grateful for the opportunities they have received and the support they have received along the way. They recognize that they are not alone in their journey and are thankful for the contributions of others. Their humility keeps them grounded and approachable, enabling them to connect with others on a deeper level and build meaningful relationships.

5. **Long-term Vision:** Champions who are selfless often have a long-term vision that extends beyond personal gains. They think beyond immediate gratification and are willing to invest their time, energy,

and resources in initiatives that have a lasting positive impact on others and the world around them. They are willing to delay personal rewards in pursuit of a greater cause or purpose. Their selflessness allows them to make decisions that align with their long-term vision, rather than seeking short-term gains.

6. **Personal Growth and Learning:** True champions understand that personal growth and continuous learning are essential for making a meaningful impact on others. They are committed to their own growth and development, as it allows them to better serve others. They constantly seek to improve their skills, expand their knowledge, and enhance their abilities in order to better contribute to the needs of those they serve.

In conclusion, selflessness is a defining characteristic of true champions. It involves serving others, practicing empathy and compassion, embracing a collaborative spirit, cultivating humility and gratitude, having a long-term vision, and prioritizing personal growth and learning. By being selfless, champions are able to make a positive impact on the lives of others, build meaningful relationships, and create a legacy that goes beyond personal achievements.

5.2 True Champions are the Honest Persons

Honesty is a fundamental quality of true champions. It encompasses being truthful, transparent, and maintaining integrity in all aspects of life. In this segment, we will explore why honesty is crucial to becoming a true champion and how it contributes to their overall character and success.

1. **Trust and Respect:** True champions understand that trust and respect are earned through honesty. They value the trust and respect

of others and know that it is a vital foundation for any meaningful relationship, whether it's personal or professional. By being honest in their words and actions, they build a reputation as a person of integrity, someone who can be relied upon and respected.

2. **Authenticity and Genuine Connections:** Champions who are honest are authentic and genuine in their interactions with others. They are not afraid to be themselves and express their true thoughts and feelings. This authenticity enables them to build deep and meaningful connections with others, as people are drawn to their sincerity and trustworthiness. They are not afraid to share their successes, failures, and vulnerabilities, which creates a sense of relatability and inspires others.

3. **Ethical Decision-Making:** True champions uphold ethical standards and make decisions based on what is right, rather than what is expedient. They do not compromise their principles for personal gain or short-term benefits. Their honesty guides them in making decisions that are fair, just, and in the best interest of all parties involved. They take responsibility for their actions and are willing to be held accountable for their choices.

4. **Personal Growth and Self-Awareness:** Champions who value honesty also prioritize personal growth and self-awareness. They are willing to reflect on their actions, thoughts, and beliefs with honesty, and are open to feedback and constructive criticism. They continuously strive to improve themselves and learn from their mistakes. Their honesty with themselves allows them to identify areas of improvement, and take steps towards becoming better individuals.

5. **Long-Term Success and Reputation:** Champions understand that honesty is a key component of long-term success and a positive reputation. They know that dishonesty may bring short-term gains, but it can have severe consequences in the long run. By being honest, they build a reputation as individuals of integrity and establish a foundation for sustained success in their personal and professional lives.

6. **Role Model for Others:** True champions recognize that their actions and behavior serve as a model for others, especially for those who look up to them. They understand the impact of their honesty on those around them and strive to set a positive example. They inspire and influence others to adopt similar values of honesty and integrity, creating a positive ripple effect that extends beyond their own sphere of influence.

In conclusion, honesty is a fundamental quality of true champions. It encompasses trust, respect, authenticity, ethical decision-making, personal growth, and setting a positive example for others. By valuing honesty in all aspects of life, champions build a foundation of integrity that contributes to their character, success, and positive impact on the world around them.

5.3 The Qualities & Traits That Will Make You a Champion

Becoming a champion requires a combination of qualities and traits that go beyond physical prowess or talent. It requires a mindset, attitude, and behaviors that set champions apart from others. In this segment, we will explore the key qualities and traits that will make you a champion.

1. **Determination and Resilience:** Champions possess unwavering determination and resilience. They have a clear vision of their goals

and are willing to put in the hard work, dedication, and perseverance required to achieve them. They do not give up easily in the face of challenges, setbacks, or failures, but rather see them as opportunities to learn, grow, and improve. They bounce back from failures and setbacks with renewed determination and use them as stepping stones towards success.

2. **Positive Mindset and Attitude:** Champions have a positive mindset and attitude towards themselves, others, and life in general. They believe in their own abilities and have a high level of self-confidence. They maintain a positive outlook even in the face of adversity and approach challenges with a "can-do" attitude. They are optimistic, hopeful, and resilient in their pursuit of success.

3. **Discipline and Self-Control:** Champions understand the importance of discipline and self-control in achieving their goals. They are committed to a disciplined approach to their craft, training, and preparation. They have the self-control to resist temptations, distractions, and shortcuts that may hinder their progress. They prioritize long-term success over short-term gratification and make conscious choices that align with their goals and values.

4. **Passion and Purpose:** Champions are deeply passionate about their craft, sport, or field of endeavor. They have a clear sense of purpose and a burning desire to excel. Their passion fuels their motivation, commitment, and perseverance, and they are willing to go the extra mile to achieve their dreams. They are driven by a sense of purpose that goes beyond personal gain and is fuelled by their love and dedication to their craft.

5. **Continuous Learning and Improvement:** Champions have a growth mindset and are committed to continuous learning and improvement. They are open to feedback, criticism, and self-reflection. They embrace challenges as opportunities to learn and grow, and are willing to step out of their comfort zones to push their limits. In other words, they are the opportunists, they have the patience to grab new opportunity and learn from their failures. They are proactive in seeking knowledge, feedback, and guidance to constantly improve their skills, knowledge, and performance.

6. **Focus and Mental Toughness:** Champions possess unwavering focus and mental toughness. They have the ability to block out distractions and maintain laser-like focus on their goals. They are mentally tough and resilient, able to manage pressure, stress, and setbacks effectively. They have a strong mindset that enables them to stay composed, confident, and focused even in high-pressure situations.

7. **Sportsmanship and Respect:** Champions exhibit sportsmanship and respect towards themselves, their opponents, and others involved in their field of endeavor. They compete with integrity, fairness, and respect for the rules and spirit of the game. They show respect to their opponents, coaches, teammates, and other stakeholders, regardless of the outcome. They understand that true champions not only excel in their performance, but also exemplify sportsmanship and respect in their conduct.

In conclusion, becoming a champion requires a combination of qualities and traits, including determination, resilience, positive mindset, discipline, passion, continuous learning, focus, and sportsmanship. By cultivating these qualities and traits, you can develop the mindset and behaviors that set champions apart and pave the way towards achieving your own personal and professional success.

6.0 The Psychological Mindsets Which are Necessary to Become a Champion

Achieving champion-level success goes beyond physical skills and talent; it also requires the right psychological mindsets. These mindsets are crucial for developing the mental resilience, focus, and determination needed to overcome challenges and perform at the highest level. In this segment, we will explore the psychological mindsets that are necessary to become a champion.

1. **Growth Mindset:** A growth mindset is the belief that abilities and skills can be developed through effort, learning, and experience. Champions embrace a growth mindset, seeing failures and setbacks as opportunities to learn and grow, rather than as limitations or reasons to give up. They believe that they can continuously improve and develop their skills, and they approach challenges with a curious and open-minded attitude, eager to learn and adapt.

2. **Positive Self-Belief:** Champions have a strong sense of self-belief and confidence in their abilities. They believe in themselves and their potential to achieve their goals. They have a positive inner dialogue and mindset, focusing on their strengths and capabilities rather than dwelling on their limitations or insecurities. They cultivate a positive self-image and nurture self-compassion, treating themselves with kindness, encouragement, and self-affirmation.

3. **Mental Resilience:** Champions possess mental resilience, which allows them to bounce back from setbacks and challenges. They have the ability to manage stress, pressure, and adversity effectively, without being overwhelmed or discouraged. They maintain a calm and composed mindset, even in high-pressure situations, and are able to stay focused and perform at their best, regardless of external circumstances.

4. **Goal Orientation:** Champions are goal-oriented and have a clear sense of purpose. They set challenging, yet realistic goals and work diligently towards achieving them. They have a clear vision of what they want to accomplish and create a roadmap to guide their efforts. They maintain focus on their goals, staying motivated and committed to their pursuit, and are willing to make sacrifices and put in the necessary effort to achieve them.

5. **Resilient Mindset:** Champions have a resilient mindset that allows them to bounce back from failures, setbacks, and disappointments. They view failures as learning opportunities and do not dwell on them or let them define their self-worth. They have the mental fortitude to persevere in the face of challenges and setbacks, maintaining a positive attitude and a strong belief in their abilities.

6. **Focus and Concentration:** Champions possess a high level of focus and concentration, enabling them to block out distractions and maintain unwavering attention to their performance. They are able to stay fully present in the moment, without being overwhelmed by external factors or distractions. They have the ability to tune out distractions and maintain a laser-like focus on their goals, tasks, and performance.

7. **Positive Relationship with Failure:** Champions have a healthy relationship with failure. They view failures as a natural part of the journey towards success and do not fear or avoid them. Instead, they embrace failures as opportunities to learn, grow, and improve. They use failures as stepping stones towards success and do not let them discourage or deter them from pursuing their goals.

8. **Visualization and Mental Imagery:** Champions utilize visualization and mental imagery techniques to mentally prepare for their performance. They create vivid mental images of themselves succeeding in their endeavors, which helps them build confidence, focus, and motivation. They use mental imagery to rehearse their performance, develop muscle memory, and enhance their overall readiness for their craft.

6.1 Be a Champion in Your Job Sector

Your job sector is a crucial aspect of your professional life, and becoming a champion in your field can lead to immense success and fulfilment. In this segment, we will delve into the mindset, skills, and strategies that can help you excel and become a champion in your job sector.

1. **Continuous Learning:** Champions in their job sector have a relentless thirst for knowledge and are committed to continuous learning. They stay updated with the latest industry trends, advancements, and best practices. They invest in their professional development through training, workshops, certifications, and other learning opportunities. They strive to stay ahead of the curve and are always willing to acquire new skills and expand their knowledge base.

2. **Excellence in Execution:** Champions are known for their exceptional execution skills. They pay meticulous attention to detail and deliver high-quality results consistently. They take pride in their work and hold themselves to high standards of performance. They are reliable, accountable, and committed to excellence in all their tasks and responsibilities.

3. **Problem-Solving and Critical Thinking:** Champions are adept at problem-solving and critical thinking. They approach challenges with a solutions-oriented mindset and are skilled in identifying and addressing issues effectively. They analyze situations, think critically, and come up with creative solutions to overcome obstacles. They are proactive in finding solutions rather than dwelling on problems.

4. **Leadership and Teamwork:** Champions understand the importance of leadership and teamwork in their job sector. They are skilled at leading and inspiring others, motivating their team to achieve common goals. They also excel at collaborating with colleagues and stakeholders, fostering a positive and inclusive work environment. They value diversity with inclusivity, and collaboration, recognizing that success is often a team effort.

5. **Adaptability and Resilience:** Champions in their job sector are adaptable and resilient in the face of changing circumstances. They embrace change as an opportunity for growth and are agile in adjusting their strategies and approaches accordingly. They remain resilient in the face of challenges, setbacks, and failures, bouncing back quickly and finding ways to overcome obstacles.

6. **Innovation and Creativity:** Champions are not afraid to think outside the box and are known for their innovative and creative approaches. They are constantly looking for ways to improve processes, products, or services. They bring new ideas to the table and are open to experimenting and taking calculated risks. They are not content with the status quo and are always seeking ways to push boundaries and create new opportunities.

7. **Networking and Relationship Building:** Champions understand the power of networking and relationship building in their job sector. They proactively build and maintain professional relationships, both internally and externally, to expand their network and create opportunities for growth. They are skilled at building rapport, fostering trust, and maintaining positive relationships with colleagues, mentors, clients, and other stakeholders.

8. **Positive Attitude and Professionalism:** Champions maintain a positive attitude and exhibit professionalism in all their interactions. They are known for their integrity, ethics, and professionalism in their job sectors. They approach challenges with a positive mindset, remain composed under pressure, and exhibit a high level of professionalism in their conduct, communication, and demeanor.

9. **Passion and Drive:** Champions in their job sector have a deep passion and drive for their work. They are intrinsically motivated and committed to their craft. They go the extra mile, putting in the effort and time required to excel in their field. Their passion and drive are evident in their work ethic, dedication, and perseverance in pursuing their goals.

In conclusion, becoming a champion in your job sector requires a combination of mindset, skills, and strategies. By cultivating a continuous learning mindset, striving for excellence, embracing problem-solving and critical thinking, demonstrating leadership and teamwork, being adaptable and resilient, fostering innovation and creativity, building professional relationships, exhibiting a positive attitude and professionalism, and nurturing passion and drive, you can elevate your performance and champion mindset.

6.2 Be a Champion in Your Business Sector

Becoming a champion in your business sector requires a unique set of mindset, skills, and strategies that are tailored to the competitive landscape of the business world. Here are some key psychological mindsets that can help you become a champion in your business sector:

1. **Entrepreneurial Mindset:** Champions in the business sector possess an entrepreneurial mindset, which includes a willingness to take calculated risks, embrace innovation, and be proactive in identifying and seizing business opportunities. They have a vision for their business and are willing to think creatively and take bold actions to achieve their goals.

2. **Growth Mindset:** Champions in the business sector have a growth mindset, which means they see challenges as opportunities for learning and growth. They are not afraid to fail, and they view setbacks as stepping stones to success. They are resilient in the face of adversity and are willing to adapt and pivot their strategies as needed.

3. **Strategic Thinking:** Champions in the business sector are strategic thinkers. They are able to see the big picture and think critically about the long-term direction of their business. They set clear goals, develop strategic plans, and execute them with precision. They analyze market trends, competitor strategies, and customer needs to make informed decisions and stay ahead of the competition.

4. **Customer-Centric Approach:** Champions in the business sector prioritize their customers. They understand the importance of building strong customer relationships and providing exceptional customer experiences. They listen to their customers, understand their needs, and tailor their products or services accordingly. They are responsive to customer feedback and are constantly looking for ways to improve their offerings.

5. **Leadership and Team Building:** Champions in the business sector are effective leaders and team builders. They inspire and motivate their team, provide clear direction, and empower their employees to perform at their best. They build a positive work culture, foster collaboration, and recognize and reward their team's contributions. They also surround themselves with talented individuals who complement their skills and abilities.

6. **Resilience and Adaptability:** Champions in the business sector are resilient and adaptable in the face of challenges and changes. They navigate uncertainties and setbacks with grace and composure. They are quick to adapt their strategies and approaches as needed, and they do not shy away from making tough decisions for the success of their business. They view challenges as opportunities to learn and grow, and they persevere in the face of obstacles.

7. **Continuous Innovation:** Champions in the business sector are always looking for ways to innovate and stay ahead of the competition. They embrace change and are willing to disrupt the status quo. They encourage a culture of innovation within their organization and foster creativity and idea generation. They are not afraid to experiment and take calculated risks to drive innovation and stay relevant in the fast-paced business world.

8. **Networking and Relationship Building:** Champions in the business sector understand the importance of networking and relationship building. They actively build and maintain professional relationships with partners, investors, suppliers, and other stakeholders. They leverage their networks to create business opportunities, seek advice, and gain insights into the industry. They are skilled in building rapport, establishing trust, and nurturing long-term relationships that can benefit their business.

9. **Persistence and Tenacity:** Champions in the business sector are persistent and tenacious. They do not give up easily and are willing to put in the hard work and effort required to achieve their business goals. They have a strong sense of determination and do not shy away from challenges or setbacks. They stay focused and committed to their vision, even when faced with obstacles, and they persevere until they achieve success.

10. **Financial Acumen:** Champions in the business sector have a solid understanding of financial management. They are knowledgeable about financial concepts, such as cash flow, profitability, and return on investment. They keep a close eye on their business finances, make informed financial decisions, and manage their resources

7.0 Corrupts are Not the Champions, They're the Fuels of Hellfire

You are absolutely right. Corruption is unethical and illegal behavior that undermines the principles of fairness, integrity, and transparency in business and society. Corrupt individuals and practices are detrimental to the progress and well-being of a community, and they can have severe negative consequences for individuals and organizations involved.

Champions are individuals and organizations that embody the positive mindsets and values necessary for success, while upholding high ethical standards. Champions operate with integrity, honesty, and accountability. They prioritize fairness, transparency, and ethical conduct in all their actions and decisions. They lead by example and inspire others to follow suit.

Corruption, on the other hand, is a destructive force that erodes trust, distorts competition, hinders economic growth, and undermines the social fabric of a community. It leads to unfair advantages, undermines merit-based systems, and perpetuates inequality. Corrupt practices, such as bribery, embezzlement, and nepotism, have no place in a champion's mindset or in any reputable business sector.

It is important for individuals and organizations to reject corruption in all its forms and promote ethical conduct in their business practices. Champions strive for excellence while upholding the highest standards of integrity, fairness, and transparency. They work towards creating a positive and sustainable impact on their business sector and society as a whole.

7.1 They're the Fuels of Hellfire

The statement "They're the Fuel of Hellfire" in relation to corrupt individuals is a strong metaphorical expression that highlights the grave consequences and negative impact of corruption. In many cultures and belief systems, the concept of hell is associated with punishment, suffering, and eternal damnation. As per the different religions, corrupts will be burning in the hellfire and they will be counted as the fuels of hellfire. This is the eternal believe that poses by the believers of the different religions. Referring to corrupt individuals as the "fuel of hell" underscores the serious nature of corruption and its detrimental effects on individuals, communities, and society as a whole. Corrupts may get the opportunities to make their society and country corrupted with their unjust actions but they'll definitely burn in hellfire in their eternal lives.

Corruption not only harms the immediate victims of corrupt practices, but it also undermines the social contract, erodes trust in institutions, and perpetuates inequality and injustice. It can lead to economic instability, social unrest, and a breakdown of moral and ethical values. Corruption tarnishes the reputation of organizations and countries, and undermines the progress and development of communities.

In many religious and ethical systems, honesty, integrity, and fairness are valued virtues, while corruption is seen as a violation of these principles. The metaphorical reference to corrupt individuals as the "fuel of hell" serves as a powerful reminder of the grave consequences of engaging in corrupt practices.

As individuals, it is our responsibility to reject corruption in all its forms and strive to be champions of integrity, transparency, and ethical conduct. By upholding high moral and ethical standards, we can contribute to a better and more just society, and prevent the spread of corruption that can have devastating consequences for individuals and communities alike.

7.2 Be a Champion in Your Personal Life

Becoming a champion in your personal life means taking charge of your life and making deliberate choices that align with your values, goals, and aspirations. It means prioritizing your mental, emotional, and physical well-being, and cultivating a positive and fulfilling lifestyle.

To become a champion in your personal life, here are some key principles to keep in mind:

1. **Define your purpose:** Identify what matters most to you, and set goals and priorities that align with your values and aspirations. Having a clear sense of purpose can help you stay focused and motivated, and make more intentional decisions.

2. **Cultivate self-awareness:** Understand your strengths, weaknesses, and limitations, and be honest with yourself about areas where you need to improve. Self-awareness can help you identify opportunities for growth and development, and make more informed decisions.

3. **Develop healthy habits:** Take care of your physical and mental health by eating well, exercising regularly, getting enough sleep, and managing stress effectively. These habits can help you maintain a positive mindset and improve your overall well-being.

4. **Build positive relationships:** Surround yourself with supportive and positive people who uplift you, challenge you, and inspire you

to be your best self. Nurture your relationships with family, friends, and loved ones, and cultivate a sense of community and belonging.

5. **Embrace lifelong learning:** Stay curious and open-minded, and commit to ongoing learning and self-improvement. Seek out new experiences, explore different perspectives, and challenge yourself to step outside your comfort zone.

By adopting these principles and committing to being the best version of yourself, you can become a champion in your personal life. Remember that becoming a champion is not a destination, but a continuous journey of growth, learning, and self-improvement.

7.3 Be a Champion in Your Work Life

Being a champion in your work life means excelling in your job or profession and making a positive impact on your organization, industry, and society. It means going above and beyond what is expected of you, demonstrating leadership and initiative, and delivering exceptional results.

To become a champion in your work life, here are some key principles to keep in mind:

1. **Develop your skills and expertise:** Stay up to date with the latest trends, technologies, and best practices in your field. Invest in your professional development by attending conferences, taking courses, and seeking out opportunities for growth and learning.

2. **Build strong relationships:** Build positive relationships with your colleagues, clients, and stakeholders. Communicate effectively, listen actively, and collaborate with others to achieve common

goals. Be proactive in offering help and support to others when needed.

3. **Demonstrate leadership:** Take ownership of your work and demonstrate leadership by taking initiative, being accountable, and inspiring others to do their best work. Be proactive in identifying and solving problems, and be willing to take calculated risks and make tough decisions when necessary.

4. **Deliver exceptional results:** Set high standards for yourself and strive for excellence in everything you do. Be results-driven, focus on achieving measurable outcomes, and continuously look for ways to improve your performance.

5. **Maintain a positive attitude:** Maintain a positive and professional attitude, even in challenging or stressful situations. Be resilient, adaptable, and open to feedback and constructive criticism. Cultivate a culture of positivity and collaboration in your workplace.

By following these principles and striving to be the best in your field, you can become a champion in your work life. Remember that becoming a champion is not just about achieving individual success, but also about making a positive impact on your organization, industry, and society.

7.4 Champion Might Turn into a Leader

Yes, it's true that a champion can also turn into a leader. In fact, many champions possess the qualities and skills that are essential for effective leadership. A champion is someone who excels in their field, demonstrates leadership qualities, and inspires others to follow their lead. Similarly, a leader is someone who inspires, motivates, and guides others to achieve a common goal.

Champions often possess the following qualities that are also essential for effective leadership:

1. **Vision:** Champions have a clear vision of what they want to achieve and how they want to make a difference in their field. Similarly, leaders have a clear vision of their organization's mission, goals, and values, and they inspire others to share that vision.

2. **Focus:** Champions have a laser-like focus on their goals and are willing to put in the hard work and dedication required to achieve them. Similarly, leaders are focused on achieving their organization's goals and priorities, and they inspire others to stay focused on those priorities as well.

3. **Resilience:** Champions are resilient and able to bounce back from setbacks and failures. Similarly, leaders are resilient and able to navigate through difficult times and inspire their team to do the same.

4. **Communication:** Champions are able to communicate effectively and inspire others through their words and actions. Similarly, leaders are skilled communicators who can inspire, motivate, and guide others towards a common goal.

5. **Passion:** Champions are passionate about what they do, and their enthusiasm is contagious. Similarly, leaders are passionate about their organization's mission and goals, and they inspire others to share that passion.

By cultivating these qualities and skills, a champion can easily transition into a leadership role and continue to make a positive impact in their field and beyond.

7.5 Few Examples of Modern Life Champions

There are many examples of modern life champions in various fields who have achieved great success through hard work, dedication, and perseverance. Here are just a few examples:

1. **Muhammad Ali** - Considered by many to be the greatest boxer of all time, Ali won numerous titles and awards throughout his career, including three heavyweight championships. He was known for his quick wit, his flashy style, and his unwavering confidence.

2. **Oprah Winfrey** - Winfrey is a media mogul, actress, and philanthropist who has been named one of the most influential people in the world. She overcame a difficult childhood to become the host of one of the most successful talk shows in history, and has since launched her own television network and production company.

3. **Elon Musk** - Musk is a business magnate and entrepreneur who has founded several successful companies, including Tesla Motors, SpaceX, and PayPal. He is known for his ambitious goals and his commitment to advancing science and technology.

4. **Serena Williams** - Williams is one of the greatest tennis players of all time, with 23 Grand Slam singles titles to her name. She has overcome numerous injuries and setbacks throughout her career, and is known for her fierce competitiveness and determination.

5. **Dwayne "The Rock" Johnson:** Dwayne Johnson is an American actor, producer, and former professional wrestler. He has become a successful actor and entrepreneur, and has used his platform to inspire others to achieve their goals and never give up on their dreams.

6. **Simone Biles:** Simone Biles is an American gymnast who has won numerous Olympic and World Championship titles. She has been a vocal advocate for mental health and has used her platform to raise awareness and reduce the stigma surrounding mental illness.

7. **Imran Khan**: Pakistan former world champion cricket star, Khan became the Prime Minister of Pakistan in 2018. He has been a vocal advocate for anti-corruption measures and has worked to improve the country's education and healthcare systems. He lost the no-confidence vote in 2022 against the corrupt oppositions who're backed by the Western regime to establish their puppet govt. in Pakistan. Unstoppable Imran Khan is still fighting hard by the grace of Almighty Allah against these corrupt oppositions to establish an incorruptible govt. in Pakistan.

8. **Jacinda Ardern**: Ardern is the former Prime Minister of New Zealand, had taken office in 2017. She has been praised for her compassionate leadership style and her response to the Christchurch Mosque shootings in 2019, during which she showed empathy and support for the Muslim community.

9. **Shinzo Abe:** Japan: Abe served as the Prime Minister of Japan from 2012 to 2020, during which he focused on revitalizing the country's economy and promoting international cooperation. He was also

known for his efforts to improve Japan's relationship with neighbouring countries like China and South Korea.

10. **Angela Merkel:** Merkel is a physicist who served as the Chancellor of Germany from 2005 to 2021, making her the longest-serving head of government in the European Union. She was known for her leadership during the Eurozone crisis and for her support of liberal democracy and human rights.

11. **Nelson Mandela:** Mandela was an anti-apartheid revolutionary who became the first black president of South Africa, serving from 1994 to 1999. He spent 27 years in prison for his activism before being released in 1990, and he worked tirelessly to promote peace and equality until his death in 2013.

These are just a few examples of the many champions who have achieved great success through their hard work, unwavering dedication, and perseverance

8.0 You Don't Need to Pose Extraordinary Qualities to Become a Champion

It's true that you don't necessarily need to possess extraordinary qualities to become a champion. While certain qualities and traits can certainly be helpful, it's often a combination of hard work, dedication, and a willingness to learn and grow that leads to success.

Many champions start off with humble beginnings and work their way up through sheer determination and persistence. They may not have been born with exceptional talents or abilities, but they were willing to put in the effort to develop the skills they needed to succeed.

In fact, sometimes it's the struggles and challenges we face that can help us become champions. By overcoming obstacles and persevering through adversity, we develop the resilience, determination, and perseverance that are often necessary for success.

Of course, it's important to recognize that everyone's journey is different, and what works for one person may not work for another. However, the idea that you need to possess extraordinary qualities or abilities to become a champion is often a myth. With hard work, dedication, and a willingness to learn and grow, anyone can achieve success and become a champion in their own right.

Additionally, it's important to remember that champions come in all shapes and sizes, from all walks of life, and in all areas of endeavours. Some may excel in sports, while others may excel in business, science, or the arts. The common thread that binds all champions together is their unwavering commitment to their goals and their willingness to put in the effort required to achieve them.

Another key factor in becoming a champion is setting realistic and achievable goals. While it's great to have big dreams and aspirations, it's important to break them down into smaller, more manageable steps. By setting achievable goals and working towards them consistently, you can build momentum and gain the confidence and skills you need to achieve even greater success.

Ultimately, becoming a champion is about taking action and staying focused on your goals. It's about having the courage to pursue your passions and dreams, and the persistence to overcome obstacles and setbacks along the way. While possessing certain qualities and skills can certainly be helpful, it's often the mindset and attitude of a champion that sets them apart and enables them to achieve great things.

8.1 The Daily Routine You Should Follow to Become a Champion

If you want to become a champion, it's important to develop a daily routine that will help you stay focused and productive. Here are some key elements that you might want to include in your routine:

1. **Wake up early** - Many successful people swear by the benefits of waking up early, as it gives them time to plan their day, exercise, and get a head start on their work.

2. **Exercise** - Regular exercise is important for both physical and mental health, and can help you stay energized and focused throughout the day.

3. **Plan your day** - Take some time each morning to plan out your schedule and prioritize your tasks for the day. This can help you stay organized and focused on your goals.

4. **Focus on your priorities** - Don't get distracted by minor tasks or requests that can wait. Instead, focus on the most important tasks that will help you achieve your goals.

5. **Take breaks** - It's important to take breaks throughout the day to recharge and avoid burnout. Consider taking short walks or doing other activities that help you clear your mind and refocus.

6. **Learn continuously** - Champions are always learning and seeking to improve their skills and knowledge. Make a habit of reading

books, taking courses, or seeking out other learning opportunities that can help you grow and develop.

7. **Practice gratitude** - Cultivating a mindset of gratitude can help you stay positive and motivated even in difficult times. Consider keeping a gratitude journal or taking time each day to reflect on the things you're thankful for.

8. **Surround yourself with positive influences** - The people you spend time with can have a big impact on your mindset and success. Surround yourself with supportive and positive people who can help you stay motivated and focused on your goals.

9. **Stay organized** - Keeping your workspace and schedule organized can help you stay productive and avoid distractions. Make a habit of keeping your workspace tidy, and consider using tools like calendars or task lists to help you stay on top of your schedule.

10. **Embrace challenges** - Champions don't shy away from challenges; they see them as opportunists for growth and improvement. Instead of avoiding difficult tasks or situations, embrace them as chances to learn and develop new skills.

11. **Practice self-care** - Taking care of yourself is essential for both physical and mental health. Make sure you're getting enough sleep, eating well, and taking breaks when you need them. Consider incorporating self-care practices like meditation or yoga into your routine to help you stay centered and focused.

12. **Seek feedback** - Champions are always looking for ways to improve, and feedback can be a valuable tool for growth. Don't be

afraid to ask for feedback from coworkers, mentors, or other trusted sources, and use it to guide your development and improvement.

13. **Set goals** - Champions have clear goals and a plan for achieving them. Set specific, measurable goals for yourself, and create a plan for how you will achieve them. Regularly review your progress and adjust your plan as necessary to stay on track.

By incorporating these elements into your daily routine, you can develop the habits and mindset that are necessary to become a champion not just in your work, but in all areas of your life. Remember that becoming a champion is not just about achieving success, but also about embodying the qualities and traits that make you a better person and a positive influence on those around you.

8.2 Believers are the True Champions

Believers can certainly embody the qualities and traits that are necessary to become champions. In many religious traditions, being a champion or a winner is not just about achieving success in this world, but also about following a path of righteousness and spiritual development.

For example, in Islam, believers are encouraged to strive for excellence in all areas of their lives, including their work and personal lives, but also in their relationship with Allah and their fellow human beings. They are encouraged to embody virtues like honesty, patience, humility, and compassion, and to seek knowledge and understanding of the world around them.

Similarly, in Christianity, believers are called to follow the example of Jesus Christ, who embodied qualities like selflessness, forgiveness, and love. They are encouraged to seek spiritual growth and to live their lives in service to others, striving to make the world a better place through their actions.

Whether you are religious or not, the principles of faith and spirituality can offer valuable guidance on how to live a fulfilling and meaningful life. By embodying the qualities of a true champion, like integrity, perseverance, and compassion, you can not only achieve success in your endeavors, but also make a positive impact on the world around you.

In addition to the spiritual aspect, being a believer can also provide a sense of purpose and direction in life. When you have a clear understanding of your values and beliefs, it becomes easier to make decisions and set goals that align with those values.

Furthermore, believers often have a strong sense of community and support, which can provide encouragement and motivation to pursue their goals and overcome challenges. In many religious traditions, there are opportunities to gather with like-minded individuals to pray, study, and reflect, which can provide a sense of belonging and connection.

Ultimately, being a believer and a champion are not mutually exclusive. In fact, embodying the qualities of a true champion can be seen as a way to live out one's faith and values in the world. By striving for excellence and making a positive impact on the world, believers can serve as an inspiration to others and contribute to the greater good.

It is important to note that being a believer does not automatically make someone a champion, just as not being religious does not disqualify someone from being a champion. However, for those who do find strength and guidance in their faith, it can be a powerful tool in their journey towards becoming a champion.

Some examples of believers who are also champions include athletes like Muhammad Ali, who was a Muslim, and Tim Tebow, who is a devout Christian. Both of these athletes have not only achieved great success in their respective sports, but have also used their platform to promote social justice and inspire others through their faith.

In conclusion, being a believer can provide a strong foundation for becoming a champion, as it can offer guidance on living a virtuous and purposeful life, a sense of community and support, and a way to make a positive impact on the world. However, it is ultimately up to the individual to embody the qualities of a true champion and strive for excellence in all areas of their life, whether they are religious or not.

Regardless of one's beliefs, it is important to recognize the power of faith in inspiring and motivating individuals to achieve their goals and overcome obstacles. Many people turn to their faith during difficult times, finding comfort and strength in their beliefs. This can be a powerful tool in the pursuit of becoming a champion, as it can help individuals maintain their focus and perseverance in the face of adversity.

Moreover, being a believer can also inspire a sense of humility and gratitude, recognizing that one's talents and successes are gifts from a higher power. This can prevent individuals from becoming complacent or arrogant in their accomplishments, and instead encourage them to continue striving for excellence and using their talents for the greater good.

Ultimately, the relationship between faith and championhood is a personal one, and will vary from individual to individual. However, it is clear that for those who find strength and inspiration in their faith, it can be a powerful tool in their journey towards becoming a champion in all areas of their life.

8.3 Champions are the Democratic Thinkers

Champions are not only skilled in their chosen field, but they also possess certain personal qualities that set them apart from the rest. One of these qualities is the ability to think democratically. A democratic thinker is someone who is open-minded, respectful of different opinions, and willing to engage in constructive dialogue with others.

In today's world, where there are many complex issues and differing viewpoints, it is more important than ever to be a democratic thinker. This means being able to listen to others, understand their perspectives, and work together to find common ground and solutions that benefit everyone.

Champions who possess democratic thinking skills are often successful in their personal and professional lives, as they are able to build strong relationships with others and navigate challenging situations with ease. They are also able to make informed decisions based on a variety of perspectives and take into account the needs and opinions of all stakeholders.

Examples of democratic thinkers who are also champions include politicians like Nelson Mandela and Mahatma Gandhi, who worked tirelessly to promote social justice and equality for all. They understood the importance of democratic thinking and believed in the power of collaboration and unity to achieve their goals.

To become a democratic thinker, there are several steps you can take in your daily life. Here are some suggestions:

1. **Practice active listening:** When engaging in conversations with others, make a conscious effort to truly listen and understand their perspective. Avoid interrupting or dismissing their opinions, even if you don't agree with them.

2. **Seek out diverse opinions:** Expose yourself to different viewpoints and opinions, whether it's through reading, watching or listening to news, or engaging in conversations with people from different backgrounds.

3. **Embrace collaboration:** Work with others to solve problems and find solutions. Be open to compromise and finding common ground.

4. **Respect others:** Treat everyone with respect and dignity, even if you disagree with their opinions. Avoid personal attacks or belittling others.

5. **Practice empathy:** Put yourself in other people's shoes and try to understand their experiences and perspectives. This will help you approach problems with more compassion and understanding.

Incorporating these practices into your daily routine can help you become a more democratic thinker and ultimately, a better champion in all areas of your life.

In conclusion, being a democratic thinker is an important quality for champions to possess. It allows them to work effectively with others, build strong relationships, and make informed decisions that benefit everyone. By adopting this mindset, individuals can become true champions in all areas of their life.

8.4 True Champions Assist Others Selflessly

One of the defining traits of true champions is their willingness to assist others selflessly. They understand that their success is not solely their own, and that they have a responsibility to use their talents and abilities to help those around them.

True champions know that by lifting others up, they are creating a better world for everyone. They see the potential in those around them and work tirelessly to help them reach it. Whether it's offering words of encouragement, providing mentorship, or lending a helping hand, true champions are always looking for ways to assist others in achieving their goals.

But their assistance is not driven by selfish motives. They don't seek recognition or praise for their actions. Instead, they find joy in seeing others succeed and grow. They know that true fulfillment comes not from personal achievements, but from making a positive impact on the lives of others.

So, if you want to become a true champion, make it a priority to assist others selflessly. Look for ways to give back to your community, mentor those who are just starting out, and lend a helping hand whenever you can. By doing so, you'll not only be making a positive impact on those around you, but you'll also be embodying the qualities and traits of a true champion.

Moreover, assisting others selflessly not only benefits those who receive it, but it also benefits the champion themselves. By helping others, champions develop a sense of purpose and fulfilment that goes beyond personal achievements. They create meaningful connections with those around them, and these connections can lead to opportunities for growth and advancement.

In addition, true champions understand that we all have a responsibility to give back to our communities and make the world a better place. They use their talents and abilities to create positive change, whether it's through volunteering, activism, or social entrepreneurship.

So, if you want to be a true champion, remember to always look for opportunities to assist others selflessly. Whether it's in your personal life, your career, or your community, there are countless ways to make a positive impact on those around you. And by doing so, you'll not only be embodying the qualities and traits of a true champion, but you'll also be making a lasting impact on the world around you.

9.0 Follow SMART Model to Be a Champion

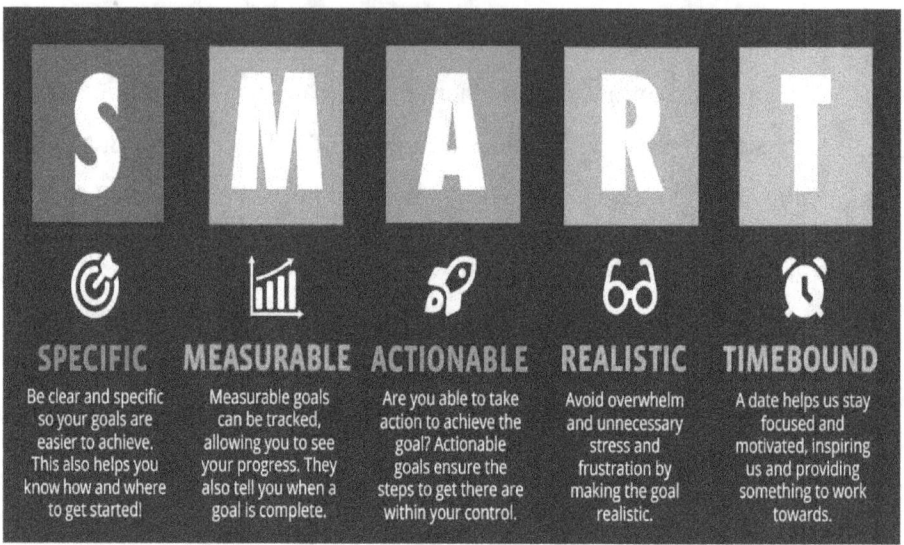

One effective way to become a champion is to follow the SMART model. This model stands for Specific, Measurable, Achievable, Relevant, and Time-bound. By setting goals that meet these criteria, you can increase your chances of success and become a champion in your chosen field.

9.1 Specific

First, set specific goals that are clear and well-defined. Vague goals are difficult to achieve, so it's important to be specific about what you want to accomplish. For example, if you want to become a champion athlete, you might set a goal to run a 5 KM race in under 20 minutes.

9.2 Measurable

Next, make sure your goals are measurable. This means that you should be able to track your progress and measure your success. For example, if your goal is to increase your sales performance, you might measure your success by tracking the number of new customers you bring in each week.

9.3 Achievable

Your goals should also be achievable. While it's important to challenge yourself, it's also important to set realistic goals that you can actually achieve. Setting unattainable goals can lead to frustration and disappointment.

9.4 Relevant

Your goals should also be relevant to your overall objectives. In other words, they should align with your long-term goals and aspirations. For example, if your long-term goal is to become a successful entrepreneur, your short-term goals should be focused on building the skills and knowledge you need to achieve that goal.

9.5 Time-bound

Finally, make sure your goals are time-bound. This means that you should set a specific deadline for achieving your goals. This will help you stay focused and motivated, and it will give you a sense of urgency to take action.

By following the SMART model, you can set goals that are specific, measurable, achievable, relevant, and time-bound. This will help you stay on track, measure your progress, and ultimately become a champion in your chosen field.

10.0 Conclusion

In conclusion, becoming a champion is not an easy task, but it is possible with the right mindset and actions. This book has explored various aspects of being a champion, including adopting a healthy lifestyle, practicing selflessness, honesty, and democratic thinking. We have also discussed the importance of religious beliefs and the role they can play in becoming a true champion.

Becoming a champion is not just a title, it's a way of life. It requires unwavering dedication, commitment, and an unrelenting desire to be the best. It's not an easy road, and there will be moments of doubt, fear, and uncertainty. But if you're willing to put in the work and make sacrifices, the rewards can be immeasurable.

Imagine waking up each day with a sense of purpose and direction, knowing that you're making a difference in the world. Imagine having the strength to face any challenge, and the resilience to bounce back from failure. That's what being a champion is all about.

It's about living a life of integrity, honesty, and selflessness. It's about lifting others up and empowering them to achieve their dreams. It's about being a leader, not just a follower. And it's about leaving a positive impact on the world.

So, if you're ready to take on the challenge, to push yourself to new heights, and to live a life of purpose, then start today. Embrace the qualities and traits of a champion, and let them guide you on your journey. The road may be tough, but the destination is worth it. You have the potential to become a true champion, so go out there and make it happen.

By following the guidelines and suggestions presented in this book, you can cultivate the necessary traits and qualities to become a champion in all areas of your life. Whether it's in your personal relationships, work, or business, adopting a champion's mindset will help you overcome challenges and achieve your goals.

Remember, being a champion is not just about winning, but also about living a fulfilling life with purpose and integrity. So, strive to become the best version of yourself and make a positive impact on those around you. With dedication and hard work, you too can become a champion.

About the Author

Ghazi Mokammel Hossain

Ghazi Mokammel Hossain, known as G. Hossain, is a talented wordsmith who weaves captivating tales that leave readers spellbound. As a freelance writer, he has honed his craft, creating not only books but also articles, research papers, and creative pieces that showcase his insatiable curiosity and creative prowess. From an early age, Ghazi Mokammel Hossain excelled in academia, acing exams and pursuing higher education with a thirst for knowledge. He holds a Bachelor's degree in Business Administration and a Master's degree in Disaster Management, along with additional certifications in Social Compliance & CSR.

In 2013, Ghazi Mokammel Hossain made his mark in literary history with his debut book, "IPv4 IP6 Technology & Implementation," published on Amazon Kindle and Createspace. Since then, he has continued to publish a diverse range of books on various subjects, earning award nominations for his fictional and non-fictional works. One of his outstanding novels, "Survival of USA: Emergence of Unknown Defenders," published in 2022, has mesmerized readers with its gripping tale of suspense and intrigue. His writing is a symphony of words, leaving a lasting impact on readers long after they've turned the last page.

Beyond writing, Ghazi Mokammel Hossain indulges in his favorite hobbies, including sports such as football and cricket, gaming, and outdoor adventures like biking and walking. His thirst for knowledge extends beyond books, as he eagerly devours research papers and scholarly articles.

With his pen as his sword and his words as his armor, Ghazi Mokammel Hossain continues to push the boundaries of literature, leaving readers in awe of his boundless creativity. His words are a symphony that echoes in the hearts of readers, and his passion for storytelling knows no bounds. A true wordsmith, he is a force to be reckoned with in the world of literature.

Also by G. Hossain & GM Publishers
(Including Purchase Link QR Code)

The Last Reds: Era of Injustice & True Justice – July 15, 2023 by G. Hossain

Quick & Easy Burger, Sandwich Recipes: 50 Delicious Mouthwatering Healthy Traditional, Vegan Burger & Sandwich Recipes Book - April 11, 2023 by G. Hossain

How to Promote Your Supermarket Products: Marketing Practices of the Supermarkets in the Changing Global Business Environment - April 10, 2023 by G. Hossain

IPv4 IPv6 Technology and Implementation: Third Edition - March 15, 2023 by G. Hossain

Survival of USA: Emergence of Unknown Defenders - February 27, 2022 by G. Hossain & Md. Fazle Mubin

The Brave Parrot of Jungle: Second Edition - December 19, 2021by S.T. Ara

Climate Change: The Roles of Govt., Industries, NGOs, Political Parties, Media & Public - July 30, 2021 by G. Hossain & Md. Fazle Mubin

Notebook: Colored Retro Styled Blank Line Pocket Notebook Paperback – July 25, 2021 by G. Hossain

Lightweight Cryptography & Crypto Currency: Possibilities & Challenges in the Modern Business Context - July 12, 2021 by G. Hossain, Sadman Alam, Md. Fazle Mubin

The Author: Revealer of Unseen Truth (Day to Dusk Book 1)- December 17, 2019 by G. Hossain

Quick & Easy Pickling Cookbook: With Chutney, Jelly & Sauce Recipes- December 11, 2018 by S.T. Ara

True Friends- July 20, 2018 by G. Hossain & MD. Fazle Mubin

Marketing Strategy & Research: In the Context of Different Organizations- November, 2017 by Ghazi Mokammel Hossain & MD. Fazle Mubin

Supermarket Management Practices: In the Changing Economic Environment- November, 2016 by Ghazi Mokammel Hossain

Anwar: Emergence of Unknown Defenders- August 10, 2016 by Ghazi Mokammel Hossain

The Survival of USA – Part Two: A Novel - August, 2016 by Ghazi Mokammel Hossain & MD. Fazle Mubin

Business Environment: Theoretical & Organizational Aspects – July,2016 by Ghazi Mokammel Hossain

The Survival of USA - Part One: A Novel – March, 2016 by Ghazi Mokammel Hossain, MD. Fazle Mubin & Pranjal Rahman

Enterprise IPv6 for Enterprise Networks- December, 2015 by Ghazi Mokammel Hossain & Fathe Mubin

Heart of Democracy: A Versatile Poetry Book - Aug 28, 2015 by Ghazi Mozammel Hossain

The Brave Parrot of Jungle - Dec 11, 2014 by S.T. Ara & Gulshan Ahmed

The Mirror of Religion - Jul 19, 2015 by Ghazi Mozammel Hossain & Richard Marks

Introduction to Network on Chip Routing Algorithms - Oct 4, 2014 by Ghazi Mokammel Hossain

Ebola Epidemic: A Detail Survival Guide From Ebola Virus Disease Outbreak - Oct 25, 2014 by Ghazi Mokammel Hossain

Fundamental of API Based Financial Engineering - Oct 17, 2014 by Ghazi Mokammel Hossain

IPv4 IPv6 Technology and Implementation - Nov 2, 2013 by Ghazi Mokammel Hossain & GM Hossain

For more information, please visit Amazon Author Central

GM Publishers

https://www.amazon.com/Ghazi-Mokammel-Hossain/e/B00GGATR2K

https://www.gmpublishers.com/